WE RUN UP!

WE RUN UP!

Learning to embrace life's challenging moments and what running hills with my dad taught me.

Andrea Sayers
Dennis Reeder

ISBN: 1508536570

ISBN-13: 978-1508536574

CONTENTS

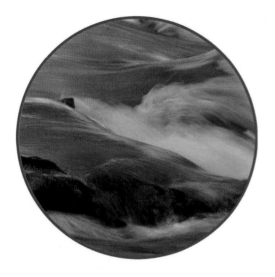

ACKNOWLEDGMENTS

My father and I are grateful to so many who have inspired and influenced the pages you hold in your hands. We may have put the words on the pages, but we want to recognize some very important people that influenced and helped along the way.

- Jan Reeder, my mother, provided numerous editing, marketing, and other book specific tasks that have enhanced the finished product. However, more than that, she endured countless hours of her husband's absence as my dad and I were absorbed in writing and editing. I know the departure from our normal family routine must have been exasperating; thank you mom. Thank you for graciously giving dad and me a "leave of absence" during our writing mania.

- Scott Sayers, my husband, never bats an eye at all my crazy ideas. He's always there to encourage and support me. Living with a runner takes a special person. His enduring patience with my smelly clothes and early morning alarm clocks are just the beginning of his role in this book. You truly are the "wind beneath my wings".

- Connor, Kaitlyn, Christopher and Kennedy, my children, I feel blessed every day to be your mother and draw inspiration from your abundance of energy. Thanks for being my biggest supporters in all my endeavors.

- Wendell Daguno, Thanks for teaching me how to master the crazy world that is social media and marketing, and helping us to share our book with the masses.

- Cindy Cloninger and Brenda Ransom, for being my rocks, my sounding boards and my best friends. For always giving me honest feedback and always being up for an adventure.

- Sole Sisters Canada trip, for being my partners in far away runs, including the Canada trip that required me to increase my hill training, and ultimately, led to my Dad and I running all those glorious hills. Sole Sisters is a small group of women with the same goal of health, love of running and adventure that unite every year to take a bucket list running trip somewhere amazing and share a week of trail running fun, gourmet cooking, playing like kids and laughter.

- Michael Candler, for teaching me the most valuable lesson about life through a simple question and always being willing to sing a little Roxanne on the trails.

- Holly Huckabee, for her invaluable editing contributions during a very busy period of her life. Thank you Holly.

Lastly, thanks to all the countless runners and competitors over the years that have coached, mentored and inspired both of us. You have helped us to push beyond our limits and urged us to become not only better runners, but better people.

One becomes a champion by embracing the hill as an opportunity for growth.

FORWARD
BY DENNIS REEDER

"No, we go up!" These words spoken by Lasse Viren (Finland's legendary Olympic runner) stopped us in our tracks. I, and about ten of my fellow Nike employees (including the then Nike President) were escorting Mr. Viren as our guest on a lunch time run that followed the Nike running trail around the World Headquarters Campus in Beaverton, Oregon. The 2 mile bark-chip trail meanders through trees and open spaces, and occasionally challenges the runner to climb steep hills that connect overpasses for the various entrances to the Nike Campus. It was at our first encounter with one of these steep hills that we decided to take a shortcut around the hill in deference to our guest, the running legend. After all, we knew the campus best and how to make the run easier for him.

Our guest, Lasse Viren, was the same runner that Steve Prefontaine had so ferociously battled in that epic 1972 Olympic 5000 meter race. He then went on to win four Gold Medals in the 1972 & 1976 Olympic Games. And now, twenty years later, we were giddy with delight at our good fortune to be running in his company. This is a runner's dream!

Mr. Viren's words, "No, we go up," brought us back to reality like the proverbial two by four across the forehead. We looked behind us and saw our guest waiting for us at the bottom of the hill and immediately felt rebuked and reprimanded. In an instant we felt ashamed and silly for presuming that a runner of Mr. Viren's caliber would appreciate short cutting away from the challenge of the hill. And then, as if recognizing our uneasiness, he pointed his finger toward the hill and tactfully softened his admonition in the form of a question; "We Run Up, YES?" To which we responded in chorus, "Yes, Yes, Yes!" Immediately we altered our course directly back to the hill. Needless to say, we ran up every hill on our run that day.

Since then I have never forgotten the lesson of the hill. In Lasse Viren's broken English way, he taught us that one becomes a champion by embracing the hill as an opportunity for growth. The hills we encounter in life (problems, setbacks, injury, disappointment, etc.) can work for our good in three specific ways if we will see them as opportunities: 1. Hills cause many people to quit, leaving more opportunity for us if we will keep going. 2. Hills cause us to realize our need for support and ask others for help. It is easier to run the hill when accompanied by a team of encouragers. 3. Hills cause us to refine our technique and sharpen our skills, which increases our competitive capacity.

I am now in retirement from the corporate world, but not from life. I am staying with this great adventure as long as I can. I have always said that *I want to die young, as late as possible!* - And running has been one of my means to this end.

I started running when I was 15 years old — more than 45 years ago, before running was cool and socially accepted. I have been blessed to be able to continue running into my 60's and I am even more blessed that my daughter Andrea enjoys running with me. She is now a mother of four and owns a fitness gym with her husband. I am both amazed and thrilled that she creates time in her busy schedule to run a hill workout with me every week. These workouts have become more than a training exercise; they have evolved into a "sort of" laboratory for our souls. Somehow in the midst of burning lungs, straining muscles, and rushing endorphins we stumble into insights that we call "Ahas," which challenge us to increase our competitive capacity for life. Some time ago, Andrea began writing some of these in her Facebook Blog and immediately began receiving responses and requests for more.

That is how this book was born. What you hold in your hands is a compilation of some of our many running adventures together, the love we have for running and the epiphanies--"*Ahas*"--we have gathered along the way. While we have written the book together, we have written it with Andrea's voice to make it easier to read. We hope you enjoy reading it as much as we have enjoyed writing it. Come; join us as, "WE RUN UP."

Life is
not an
individual
sport, it
is a team
adventure!

14

WE STRIVE TOGETHER

I love mornings when I look out my window or drive down our neighborhood street and see that familiar running style that I can instantly spot from a distance. I know this running style well because it was ingrained in me from early childhood, spending countless hours on tracks, at races, and being coached on it by his side. It is a beautiful thing to watch, as if every muscle in his body is in perfect symphony with the pavement below. There is no perceived struggle as he gracefully yet powerfully slices through the air as a cohesive unit. He learned years ago as an elite runner that to strive forward at an explosive rate it takes a synchronized effort from his entire body.

On one particular Wednesday morning driving through our neighborhood, headed for town, I spotted that effortless, bounding running style of my dad in the distance. As I pulled up alongside him, I rolled down my window to ask what I had wanted to ask for several days. I wanted to know if he would be interested in doing weekly hill repeats with me as preparation for my upcoming "Sole Sisters" running trip to Canada. After he responded with an enthusiastic "sure, let's do it" we agreed on a time, and our weekly Thursday Morning "Daddy-Daughter Run" was born.

We both run multiple times a week because that is who we are, what we do and what we have done for years. It is not like either of us did not already run hills and hill repeats, but there is something about sharing the hills with a partner that makes even the biggest hill feel smaller and less intimidating. Somehow, just hearing the rhythmic breathing and footfall of someone bearing the same journey makes the steps more doable. There is a resolve that comes from striving together as a team to get the job done, knowing that in this moment the person next to you understands what you are feeling. There is an unspoken comradery urging us to keep going through the steepest, most challenging section of the hills: the mindset of "I'm not quitting if you're not!" Then there are the shared glances from each other at the top that says we owned that hill and together we are victorious!

Does this sound like the picture perfect running scenario? Well, not every Daddy-Daughter Run has had this result. There have been days when we showed up for the hills tired and sore from previous workouts. Days when the hills have chastised us and begged us to throw in the towel and when our legs simply have not shown up to the party. On those days, we relied heavily on our commitment to each other to show up. We individually had to recruit efficiencies from our bodies that we normally took for granted on other days when we felt stronger. Breathing, arm swing, and body posture demanded more attention when the pressure of the hill seemed to debilitate all sense of technique and rhythm. But we found we could do it if we recruited these individual components into a team effort. "Swing 'em & breathe" became our mantra to help us get up and over our hills. Even though our legs felt dead, we discovered that they would follow our arms if we would keep them swinging. On these tough days we learned to run with our arms and found that they could carry us over the hill!

So often in life when we attempt to overcome challenges by ourselves, fear creeps in and causes us to lower our expectations and our resolve. We stand at the bottom of our hill with lofty goals but are afraid to start the climb because it seems insurmountable. *We get stopped by the start!*

Well, I have news for you: we were not made to go it alone!! You were not put here to figure out how to climb the hills and descend through the valleys of life by yourself. By sharing your challenges with others you will find the inspiration, motivation, encouragement, and accountability you need to run your hill. It is okay to lean on a friend or a loved one. It is ok to say "I need you; I want you by my side." It is important to ask for help.

I remember during the cool down of one of our workouts my dad reminded me of the humorous way my grandpa (his dad) would ask for help. With a wry smile he would make his request in the form of a statement; *"I can do this all by myself if you'll help me!"* – Wow! How appropriate that is for running! We run as individuals, but our success comes in the company of others. We love to compete but our competitive capacity is enhanced in collaboration with others. We can take inspiration from the word itself: *Compete*, which comes from two Latin roots, **com** (CUM) and **petere** (PET-ER-AH), which means *"to strive together"*.

What began as having my dad help me train for a running adventure became the adventure. With each passing Thursday morning we became stronger, and so did our relationship. We talked about everything during our runs, and often our conversations would end up with deep significant meaning about the adventure we call life.

AHAS:

- ➤ Don't let the start stop you!
- ➤ Life is not an individual sport, it is a team adventure!
- ➤ The degree to which we experience success in life is the degree to which we are willing to ask for help!
- ➤ The Latin root of the word <u>compete</u> is *com petere;* meaning *"to strive together."*

Our thinking and speaking directly affect our level of energy and enthusiasm.

"Let's keep it fun!" - If my dad and I were to carry a banner over our heads, during our runs, this is what you would read. It is another one of Dad's familiar sayings and a motto he lives by. He even goes so far to say that we should not refer to our runs as "workouts", "they should be called 'Playtime!'" He changes "speed workout" to "speed play," and we don't run "hill workouts," we "play on the hills" or "dance with the hills."

I have learned that this is more than a play on words or his attempt to be clever. He has taught me that the words we use reveal how we think about our run and determine the level of energy we bring to it. For example: Using the term "speed **work**out" promotes a completely different energy than using the term "speed **play**." Both can be used to describe the same activity but set up a whole different climate of thinking. By using the term "speed **play**" we are more likely to bring

KEEP IT FUN

you finish a tiring day of work and then look forward to doing something fun with your family or friends later in the evening. Now granted, much of your energy boost is due to the change in your environment. But that does not change the fact that your energy is there! Think about the burst of energy you get during work when your thoughts briefly take you to the evening of fun. You can experience a little rush of energy at work just by entertaining that brief moment of anticipated fun.

Our speaking and our thinking directly affect our energy level. Experiment with it at work, or play with it during your next challenging training run or race. Try tapping into your deeper reservoir of energy for running and life by approaching each as a game or adventure.

Remember, we generally will play harder than we work. So pick up your running shoes and let's go play. *Let's keep it fun!*

higher energy to the training activity because we all know that *"we play harder than we work!"*

Think about the different level of energy and enthusiasm you can generate just by changing the way you think. See if you can recall how children bring lower levels of energy to their chores as opposed to the higher energy they give to their hours of play. For that matter, think about yourself. Think about how your energy rises when

AHAS:

➢ We play harder than we work.

➢ Our thinking and speaking directly affect our level of energy and enthusiasm.

WHERE THE GRASS IS GREENER

Long runs, easy runs, tempo runs, hill repeats, heart rate training, fartlek, Lydiard hills, intervals, HIIT, Yasso 800's--the list of workouts for a runner to choose from seems endless. Being in the fitness industry exposes me to numerous athletes and their strong convictions about training. I often find myself being privately challenged and wondering what kind of training is right for me.

During one of our runs, my dad listened patiently as I continued describing my dilemma. "My challenge is more than just trying to figure out my training approach; there is something deeper going on," I explained. "When I see my running friends doing workouts different from mine I often think they may know something I don't and I might be missing something; like I am missing out on some sort of fitness party! Sometimes it feels almost like I get a little jealous of them and I will start doing their workouts. And then I will come across someone else doing something different and I will switch to what they are doing. I feel like I am in a constant state of trying to do it all to keep up with everybody else. When I realize that I cannot, I start feeling like less of a runner; like I should remove the bumper stickers from my car because I am 'not worthy.'"

> We betray the authenticity of our experience and potential when we compare ourselves to others and try to live according to their style.

Dad thought about my dilemma. He chimed in: "Sounds like you may *be chasing the greener grass, comparing* and *competing* instead of *celebrating.*" "What do you mean?" I asked. He went on to share three key points.

First: "Ask yourself if adding all those different workouts into your training routine would be consistent with your current goals." He explained that "while the various workouts of others may be good, they are only worthwhile when done within the context of a complete training program working toward a goal." He explained that we make a mistake when we compare our training with someone else's because the other person may have completely different goals, priorities and time constraints. We betray the authenticity of our running experience and potential when we compare ourselves to other runners and start running in their footsteps.

Second: "Comparing ourselves to others opens the door to feelings of inferiority and pride. If we assess that we are not as good as another person, we may develop feelings of being inferior to them. If we assess that we are better, we may become full of ourselves and become prideful. Both inferiority and pride are counterproductive to maintaining healthy relationships. They are the fruit of relating with others as competitors instead of friends. Perhaps a better way is to simply celebrate everybody's differences instead of trying to mimic or compete with them.

Third: "It is easy to get caught up in chasing the 'greener grass on the other side,' thinking that others have the inside track or advantage that we are missing. But most often the grass isn't greener on the other side. In fact, the reality is that, **the grass is greener where we water it!**"

I learned a valuable running and life lesson that morning. Comparing ourselves with others is unwise. It is far better to compare ourselves to ourselves, to adequately assess our abilities and our goals. We should not allow ourselves to be side tracked by what others are doing and think we should do it too. Instead, we should recognize their effort and give them a cheer. Then we should keep doing our thing, confident in our plan and certain of what we want to achieve.

AHAS:

> We betray the authenticity of our *experience and potential* when we compare ourselves to others and try to live according to their style.

> The grass is not always greener on the other side; *it's greener where we water it!*

The willingness to prepare is more important than the desire to succeed.

WHAT WAS I THINKING

For those who have ever experienced a run where every footfall signals a wave of regret for choices made before the run, this story is especially for you. CAUTION: Before reading any further, be forewarned that the story you are about to read is true, and it is not pretty.

It all started on Wednesday, the day before my usually scheduled Thursday run with my dad. I was finishing a series of coaching sessions with a 15 year old girl who was trying to improve her speed on the track. Although she had been showing steady improvement, today found her still falling just short of her goal for the 100 yard sprint. Sensing her frustration, I decided to run the next 100 yard sprint with her to help her meet the mark. While my intent was noble there were clearly several things wrong with this decision: 1. I am not a fast sprinter. 2. I was not warmed up. 3. I am 35 years old, not 15. – Well, she hit her time, and I PULLED MY QUAD MUSCLE. *Way to go Andrea!* I said to myself. - WHAT WAS I THINKING!? - There is more…

…Later, on that same day, as I limped up my driveway from the car, I discovered that my order of some yummy snacks had been delivered to my doorstep. These were snacks for an upcoming vacation and I could not wait to open the package and check them out. Naturally I had to be the doer of good things and make sure the snacks were edible. So, I opened them and began taste testing. I must say that I did a very thorough inspection because by evening time I discovered that half of the snacks had disappeared! I ate those snacks as if it was the last chance I would ever have to eat. I paused to briefly consider how this would play out in my run in the morning. But the temptation of the dark chocolate covered almonds and cranberries were just too powerful and I went back for more. - WHAT WAS I THINKING!? – There is more…

…Flash forward to Thursday morning; I am now getting ready to run with my dad and regretting every cursed pretty little snack bag now sitting empty on my kitchen counter. Their contents are still weighing heavy and growling in my stomach as a persistent reminder of my indiscretion. Oh, and my quad? Yeah, it is talking to me too; it was tight and sore. But I figure a little muscle rub would work the miracle I needed. By now I realize that my hobbling around the house in a sugar coma has caused me to run behind schedule for my appointed running date with my dad. So I quickly throw on my running clothes; slather my sore leg with a glob of high powered blue rub that smells so potent it could double as a decongestant, and I bolt out the door! – WHAT WAS I THINKING?! – After a few minutes into the run I realized that I WAS NOT THINKING. I had forgotten to wash the muscle rub off of my hands! I discovered this critical error in judgment immediately after my first attempt of wiping sweat from my eyes. YIKES! Now I could not see!

What a miserable run that was. I will never forget it. I finished the workout but not without a struggle. Throughout the entire run I wished that I could go back and undo my earlier impulsive decisions. I experienced a hard lesson about the importance of preparation and self-discipline. I learned that living reactively in the moment, without consideration of future consequences, will more than likely undermine my goals, AND IT CAN BE PAINFUL!

A few days later, after I was feeling better, my dad and I reflected back on my miserable experience. We observed that my *desire* to have a good "Daddy-Daughter Run" had been sacrificed to other short term impulsive wants. We explored the difference between *desiring* success and *preparing* for success. Having the desire to win is not anything special, everybody wants that. Wanting to win is only the starting point; it's when the wanting turns into passion accompanied by preparation that the magic starts happening.

Passionate desire is the spark that ignites the fire to persevere and do the disciplined work of preparation. Without focused self-disciplined preparation, the desire to win is reduced to futility. I remember someone saying that, *"failing to prepare is preparing to fail!"* That was my experience. I had taken my workout for granted and failed to make choices that would prepare me to have a good run. I WAS NOT THINKING! I was living impulsively and reactively. I ultimately paid the price for choosing short term pleasure over my more important long term goal.

Since that miserable run I have become more proactive in my approach to training. I have learned to filter my choices through the longer range perspective of goals I want to achieve. I warned you up front that this was not a pretty story. In fact, it was an ugly story for me to endure. But it has concluded with lessons learned and a happy ending. I have discovered that *my willingness to prepare is more important than my desire to succeed*. I have discovered the magical power of focused preparation.

AHAS:

➢ Failing to prepare is preparing to fail.

➢ *Passionate* desire is the spark that ignites the fire to persevere and do the disciplined work of preparation.

➢ The willingness to prepare is more important than the desire to succeed.

Before my husband and I entered our marriage, we visited a marriage counselor to help us get started with a solid foundation. During our brief time with him, he shared something that stuck with us (*in fact we were so impressed that we had it engraved on our wedding rings!*) He said, "Most people say, '*I will believe it when I see it.*' But I say you need to **believe it to see it!**" He explained that the beliefs and values we hold about our marriage determine our marriage experience. In other words, he was saying that our beliefs form the foundation of our being and doing (our experience). Without belief we are like ships without a rudder--liable to drift wherever the currents and winds of life choose to take us. At that time, I understood the counselor's point to be about keeping our belief and trust in each other fresh and alive beyond the immediate moment of expressing our vows. But it was not until many years later, during a *"Daddy-Daughter Run,"* that I came to understand the deeper implication of the power of belief.

We were finishing our workout, running our cool down, when I casually started sharing my long range running goals with my Dad. I remember feeling a little sheepish (almost embarrassed) when I heard myself expressing them out loud. Because they seemed so fantastically beyond my reach I remember asking my Dad if he thought I could achieve them. "Do you believe it is possible?" I asked. I will never forget his response. *"It does not matter what I believe. What matters is what you believe!"* There it was again; I remembered the marriage counselor and the engraved statement on my wedding ring. I started sensing that there may be something even deeper about the power of belief that I had not tapped yet.

I pressed my Dad to say more. He explained that pursuing goals based upon someone else's belief would be like asking someone else to eat for you with the expectation that your appetite will be satisfied. In other words, our

> *Belief is the catalyst that gets us started and the motor that keeps us moving.*

individuality is uniquely distinct. No one else can eat for us, or *believe* for us. Basing our goals on somebody else's belief leaves our goal within the realm of *wishing*. And if our wish does not come true we can cop out by blaming the failure on the other person's belief; releasing us from accountability to ourselves. The deeper nuance I was hearing had to do with personal responsibility and accountability. Only *my belief* can produce the drive and persevering power I need to achieve my dreams. *My belief* is the glue that makes my commitment stick!

"There is more," he said. "Belief is more than just wishing for something and hoping it will come true. The world is full of unfulfilled wishes (poor grades, missed promotions, failed marriages, failed businesses, etc.) What differentiates believing from wishing is the key ingredient of *ACTION*. When we proactively pursue our wishes and dreams we set compelling forces in motion toward the new reality we believe can be ours. Think about it this way: if we do not *believe* our wish or dream can come true, then we will not waste our time acting on it. It is when we start acting on our dream or dreams that our belief is demonstrated and things start moving."

Since that run I began to see belief at a deeper personal level. I understand that it is *my believing that precedes my achieving!* As I start believing it, I will be on the way to seeing it.

Belief is the catalyst that gets us started and the motor that keeps us moving. I have learned to run every aspect of my life through my belief filter. I ask what I believe about my marriage, running, career, etc., and how I want each one to play out in my life. I even put this very book you are reading through my belief filter before I started writing it. I like to think of belief as working like a big magnet pulling me to the realities I want in my life; where I want to be, who I want to be, and what I want to do.

Here is how I apply the power of belief in my running:

<u>When I am training:</u> I train with a specific goal in mind. If I am training for a race, my goals will be focused on distance and time. I will run workouts that simulate that particular race. During my workouts I will run them in a way that builds my confidence. In other words, I do not beat myself up trying to prove that I can achieve my race goal. I do not follow the *"No pain, no gain"* motto. That only makes me tired and undermines my confidence. Instead, I like to finish my workouts feeling like I could do more. In this way I am creating a belief pattern that says, "I can do this!" My motto is, *"Less pain, equals more gain!"* I like to keep myself in a fresh, optimistic frame of mind, in a state of believing!

When I am racing: I believe that all of my preparation has prepared me see the results I want to achieve. I focus on being my best "head" coach by controlling how I think. I try to filter out distractions and run my race to the best of my ability, "one mile at a time."

When I am recovering: I review my race performance with an eye toward recognizing those things I did well and learning from those areas that I can improve. I use this information as I set goals for my next race. To me, the whole process I follow in training, racing, and recovering is a process of believing. It is a process of setting my running in motion toward achieving my goals. I think part of why I enjoy running so much is that it has become a sort of laboratory for observing how my goals can blossom into reality. Time and time again I keep proving to myself that *"when I believe it, I will see it."*

AHAS:

➤ Belief is the glue that makes commitment stick.

➤ My believing precedes my achieving.

➤ Belief is the catalyst that gets us started and the motor that keeps us moving.

Problems filled your plate one at a time and can be most effectively removed in the same manner.

ONE MORE AND
THEN ONE MORE

"I am a little nervous, I am not sure my legs are ready for this." I had to be honest with my dad as we stared up the long half mile incline in front of us. Lydiard hills are my nemesis and we had 4 rounds of them on today's workout menu.

Named after the famed New Zealand running coach, Arthur Lydiard, the Lydiard Hills workout is basically a round trip mile of "hell." It is run on a ½ mile gradual uphill incline; not a steep hill, but a relentless grind. The first ¼ mile is run under control but with gradual acceleration until reaching lactate threshold pace (LT pace). You know you have hit your LT when you are only able to talk in intermittent staccato-like words; forming complete sentences becomes impossible. You then hold that pace until the half mile point is reached at the top of the hill. After a brief recovery, the runner then descends back down the same ½ mile hill at the same LT pace. A round trip of completing the run up and then back down equals 1 round. We typically do 3-6 rounds in one workout session. It psyches me out! This workout is not only very physically demanding but takes a great deal of mental fortitude.

"You got this!" My dad said in his best cheerleader voice. "Do not think of the whole workout. Remember the concept of how to eat the elephant; 'one bite at a time'. Focus on this moment, this round, and let the other hills take their turn, when it is their turn. Remember to run the bottom of the hill before you run the top." Meaning, that I was to focus on what I have to do in the first quarter mile, to make sure I can run the last quarter at the set desired pace. If I took off too fast, I would peak too soon and not be able to maintain that pace and complete the workout.

After getting the first couple rounds behind me, my legs and lungs were starting to feel the toll of the workout. My dad noticed, as we recovered between rounds, that I was beginning to let the workout get in my head and it was time for a little coaching. He said, "Andy, hang in there, we have only got one more, and then one more. You can do this!" He went on to distract me from my discomfort with a story of how he learned the lesson of "chunking" from one of his friends, a Fijian Olympic runner. He described how it happened on a cold January evening between lap 18 and 19 of a 20 X 400 workout. "There were about six of us and we were each experiencing our own private "hell" trying to muster up courage for the last two laps. All of a sudden we heard our Fijian friend call out; 'hey guys, we have only got one more… and then one more! We can do this!' Uproarious laughter seized the moment until we finally regained our composure

and blasted through those last two laps." On that night, my father had learned the lesson of breaking challenges into manageable chunks, and now he was teaching me. He went on to exhort me to start breaking the hill into smaller bite size pieces. He said, "Pick land marks like the hydrant, then the mailbox, then the light pole, and so forth. Remember that 'mile by mile can feel like a trial, but inch by inch will make it a cinch.' Focus on maintaining your form; keeping arms and stride in rhythm and let the hill come to you one step at a time. RELAX." - Easier said than done! - But the lesson has stayed with me. The purpose of the workout is to learn to handle the pressure of fatigue; to feel the tired and yet find a way to keep running. Chunking the run into "one more, then one more" is a way to break it down so that it doesn't feel so overwhelming.

Reflecting back. I am reminded of similar advice I heard my father-in-law give my husband when he was going through a difficult time. "In life, when you feel crushed under the weight of numerous problems, remember that all these things viewed as a whole can feel very daunting, but when separated out and focused on individually, they will be more manageable and less overwhelming." I remember hearing his sound advice, but until I experienced it on the hill, I did not *know* it. Now I do.

AHAS:

> Mile by mile can feel like a trial, but inch by inch will make it a cinch.

> Problems filled your plate one at a time and can be most effectively removed in the same manner.

> Remember the concept of how to eat an elephant: one bite at a time!

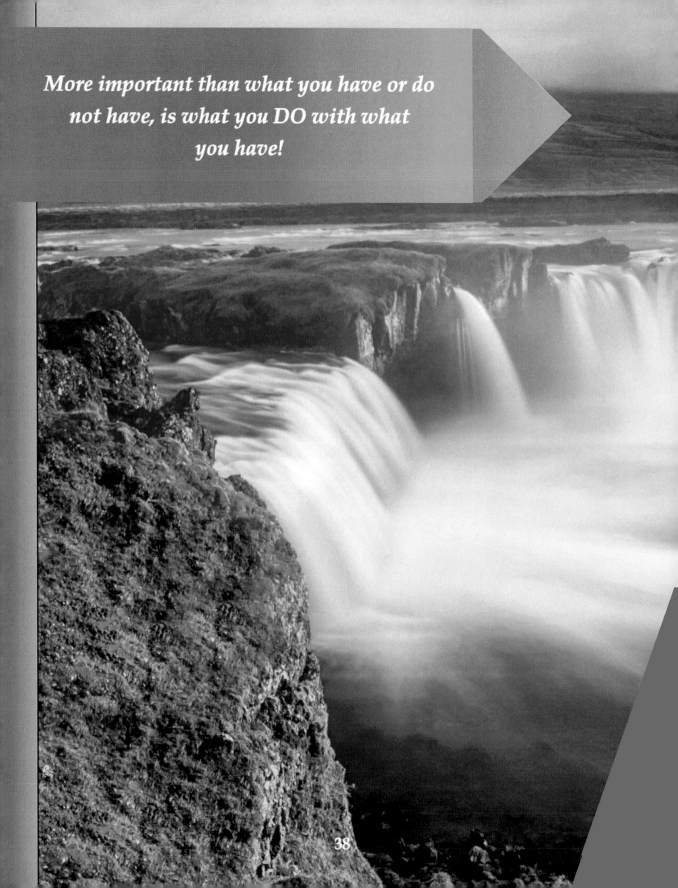

More important than what you have or do not have, is what you DO with what you have!

38

SUCCESS COMES IN A CAN

Have you ever finished your run, in failure, before you even hit foot to pavement and made excuses why you should not even lace up your shoes because you just know you are not going to find your mojo? Well, I know I have--on more than one occasion. I recall one summer morning when both my dad and I showed up with a bad case of the "can'ts".

We Run Up!

We met at our typical meeting place: the 4 way stop at the base of my dad's hill and just across the bridge from my house. We instantly started rattling off our "woe is me" stories. I shared how I was still feeling the effect of my grueling 10 mile kayak trip a couple days ago. My dad related his weariness from having carried his golf bag 18 holes the previous afternoon. Both of these things were not wild and crazy by any means, but both of us had fixated on our excuses and had built them into road blocks for our upcoming workout. Underneath our whimpering negative talk and reasons why we could not expect much out of this morning was our unspoken thought of "bagging it". Thankfully we did not, and eventually decided that since we were out and dressed for running we might as well give it a go. So we adjusted our approach to just go according to how we felt. There would be no watch glancing, no charging of the hills and no PRs set today. So, off we went, perfectly content with having let each other of the hook; the pressure was off.

We welcomed the early morning summer heat and settled in for an easy run. As we moved through our warm-up and into the first few hills we stubbornly held onto our whimpering negative chatter; as though we needed to continue justifying our easier pace. We complained about how much steeper the hills seemed, and how we could feel every one of our sore muscles. Anyone else listening might have mistaken us for a couple of nursing home patients recounting our aches and pains as badges of honor, making us worthy of throwing in the towel. But amazingly we never threw it in! We stayed with it. I do not know how, but we kept going. Usually one of us will assume the role of cheerleader to break the funk, but there was not a pom-pom to be found. But then, somewhere along the way, without a word being spoken, something clicked for both of us and our "easy" run turned into "Let's get after it." And we did, giving it the best of what we had. We stayed true to our agreement, no watch glancing or hill charging. It was just the two of us pulling

each other along with our best effort for that day. Finally, as we rounded the corner and approached our usual stopping point, my dad did glance down at his watch and made an astounding discovery. Not only had we run faster, but we had crushed our PR (Personal Record) by nearly 30 seconds. WE HAD UNDERESTIMATED OURSELVES!

We learned an important lesson that morning about the power of choice. We made a conscious decision not to force the workout in the face of our perceived weariness. We chose to give ourselves the freedom to back off and simply give the best of what we had that day. Instead of bagging the workout we focused on what we could do, rather than what we could not. In the end we learned that more important than what we HAVE or don't HAVE, is what we **DO** with what we have!

I wonder how often we do this in life. We create excuses why we are not excelling, or why we are not moving forward in our lives. We may grow weary with relationships

or careers that seemed tired and worn out. We allow negative self-talk in a way that we would never dare speak to someone else. We stop being our own best coach and instead become our own worst critic. The dirtiest four-letter word you will ever hear is "can't". We should remove it from our vocabulary. Most of the limitations we live with are self-imposed and we believe the lie that we can't. The truth is we just have not done it yet!

AHAS:

➤ Success comes in a can; not in a "can't! "

➤ More important than what you have or do not have, is what you **DO** with what you have!

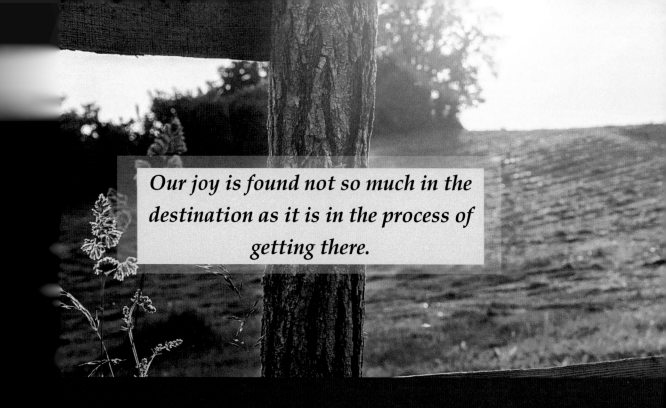

> *Our joy is found not so much in the destination as it is in the process of getting there.*

LESSONS OF THE FARM

This morning we could not resist the siren call of good old "Lila Loop Road," one of our favorite running play grounds. We find the beginning of the "Loop" about a mile from my house and follow its meandering narrow country road over gently rolling hills for 8 miles. Today we were greeted by several horses and a couple of donkeys as they peered at us from behind the pasture fence. Even though we were up early on this late summer morning we could already feel the sun's heat and were grateful for the numerous shadows covering this tree lined route.

Farmers were also up early, driving their tractors through expansive fields of green and gold harvesting their crop. Passing from farm to farm we observed the tenacious urgency with which each farmer seemed to be working and our conversation turned to the lessons of the farm playing out before us. Lessons of planting, cultivating, patience, and perseverance were in full display. We realized we were witnessing the end of a long cycle of work; the harvest, and began thinking about how the lessons of the farm apply to running and life.

A successful harvest happens by design as the farmer works in collaboration with natural laws. He begins by deciding what kind of crop he wants to harvest and then sets a plan to achieve it. He prepares the soil, making sure proper nutrients and PH are present. He plants the seed in the soil and begins the work of patiently maintaining water and cultivation while Mother Nature does the work of growing the little seed. While it does not appear that anything is happening, the farmer knows that amazing things are going on just below the surface and that over time green sprouts will break through to validate his patient effort. Patience is a key part of the formula. The novice might be tempted to push back the soil to check the seed's progress. But the farmer knows that doing so could potentially damage the crop, resulting in possible loss of the seed and the harvest. So he decides to patiently carry on day after day trusting that his work will ultimately pay off.

Somewhere, during our 8 mile run, I realized that I am a product of the "microwave" or "drive-through" generation. We have grown up with microwave ovens as a standard home appliance, putting instant gratification within reach of our finger tips. Want a hot meal? No problem. Pop it in the microwave and it is yours in less than 5 minutes. Not at home? No problem. Just pull into the drive-through lane of the nearest sandwich shop and a full meal deal is yours in less than 10 minutes.

I started thinking about how this plays out in other areas of our life as a sense of entitlement. Want a good grade in school? No problem, get a cheat sheet and bypass all that study time. And how about getting that great paying job right after graduation? You know you deserve it. What is that you say? I have got to start at the bottom and work up? But I want it now!

I started to catch on to how counterproductive this "microwave" approach would be in the natural world. The farmer was teaching me that development and growth follow an orderly progression and rhythm. Planting the seed is followed by an interlude of work before a harvest can be achieved. A baby learns to crawl before attempting to walk, and then walking precedes the ability to run. And how ludicrous would it be to ask a pregnant woman to cut her pregnancy time in half, from nine months to 4 ½?! - I was learning that we rush the rhythm and progression of nature at our peril!

That morning it dawned on me that I may be guilty of approaching my running with the "microwave mentality." Looking back I think it is possible that some of my periods of fatigue, sickness, injury, and frustration were due to my trying

to accelerate the laws of nature. I want to run longer and faster and I wanted it "NOW"! How silly I thought; I have been missing the point! The joy is not so much in the destination as it is in the process of getting there. We can be easily fooled by the lure of the destination and overlook the joy of the journey. Do not let accomplishment become a "Holy Grail." What we overcome is often more important than what we accomplish.

I will never forget today's lessons of the farm: It is in the patient struggle of the seed pushing through the soil that makes breaking through such a triumph!

AHAS:

➤ Our joy is found not so much in the destination as it is in the process of getting there.

➤ What we overcome is often more important than what we accomplish.

➤ It is in the patient struggle of the seed pushing through the soil that makes breaking through such a triumph!

BAGGAGE

I am like the kid from "Christmas Story" when I run in the cold--remember the one who cannot put his arms down? I cannot help it though; I get really cold. This morning it was 29 degrees outside and I was getting ready to go meet my dad for our weekly run. I layered myself in clothing that I thought would be sufficient; only to step out into the cold air and have it slap me into a quick about face to go back and layer on some more. I put on another jacket, heavier gloves, second pair of tights, ski hat, and my mask; the one that makes me look like I just robbed a running store! Being unfazed by my appearance, I stepped back outside; quite satisfied with my layering efforts and was off to meet my dad.

Our meeting was comical! As soon as I saw him I blurted out, "You are going to freeze!" To which he responded, "You look like the Michelin Man!" I obviously did not get my cold nature from him. He was only wearing 2 long sleeve shirts, one pair of track pants, a hat and gloves. He assured me though that he would be fine. So off we went to our warm up; he with his typical athletic stride and me with my layer induced waddle.

Our warm up proceeded in typical fashion, only colder. However, I was perfectly comfortable inside my self-made cocoon. I felt good about my decision to add more layers even with the additional weight and restricted movement. But then came the first hill and my increased effort expended to run it. I began to feel my temperature rising rapidly. By the time we hit the top I felt like we had changed to a tropical climate and I was burning up hot. "Dang, somebody turned up the heat!" I proclaimed with a whine. My dad chuckled, and said, "I feel fine, and we still have 9 hills to go!" "Ha-ha very funny." I retorted.

I was miserably uncomfortable for the rest of the run. Not only was I hot; but I was unable to get the air my lungs required due to the restrictive bulk around my chest. And my legs were like sticks; with knee flex so impaired that my legs could not generate the power needed to spring me up the hill. Yes, the thought of discarding a few layers did cross my mind. But that would put my discarded gear at risk of being picked up by some passersby. Plus, discarding would be clear admission of my poor judgment. So I struggled on to the finish, carrying my excess baggage. Tough workout for me; comical for my dad!

Later, I thought about my foolish reluctance to discard my gear. I could have easily found a place to stash it. I think my reluctance had more to do with not wanting to interrupt the workout because of my poor judgment. I did not want to interrupt the workout and have my dad wait while I rearranged my clothing for my convenience. In hind sight, I realize now that he was waiting for me anyway because of the slower pace induced by all my excess baggage. My unwillingness to stop and make some adjustments caused the quality of our workout to suffer. No big deal, it was only one workout. But I learned a big life lesson about the importance of taking care of myself. I learned that it is not selfish to stand up for what we need, and sometimes what is needed is to shed some baggage.

Going through life we can accumulate other forms of baggage without realizing it. When we are young there is the baggage that comes from people who say we are not smart enough, pretty enough, handsome enough, talented enough, or strong enough. These are lies that weigh us down with a warped sense of our potential.

There is the baggage that comes from others' imposed expectations of what is good for us. Their expectations of us become our baggage if their voice overrides our inner voice that calls us to follow a different path.

There is the baggage that comes from the fear of saying "NO" to another's request for your time. Not being able to say "NO" may be the baggage that restricts your capacity to say "YES" to your dream, or restricts your ability to say "YES" to the needs of your family. Much of the baggage we carry may come from our fear of disappointing other people and their resulting disapproval of us. We become anxious and afraid that others will not like us. Carrying the unrealistic baggage of

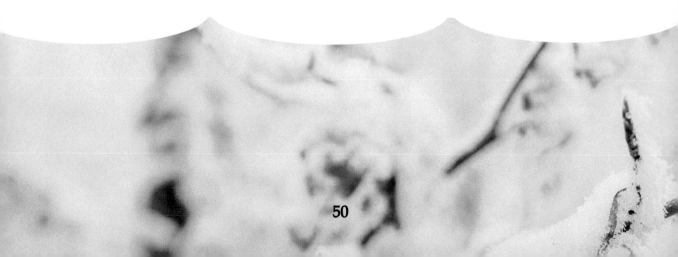

thinking we can do it all and please everyone will ultimately weigh us down and suffocate our joy.

There is the baggage of "stuff!" I am talking about toys, cars, houses, country club memberships, etc. There is nothing wrong with any of these things, unless they become symbols of our value as a person. We don't need stuff to validate our value.

The odd thing about baggage is that after we carry it for a while we get used to it and feel comfortable with it. So we keep hanging on to it even though it might not be serving us well.

So what do you think? Do you have any excess baggage you are toting around? Is there anything weighing you down; restricting your creativity, or suffocating your joy? This might be a good time to take a break and check out what you are carrying. Maybe you will decide to lighten your load!

AHAS

- ➢ Just because someone says something about me, doesn't mean it is so.

- ➢ Saying "NO" is easy when I have a bigger "YES" in mind.

- ➢ I will not allow my dreams to be held hostage to someone else's expectation of me.

- ➢ My value as a person is not symbolized by "stuff."

PERSPECTIVE

We are geared for exploration, discovery and change.

"Wow, what a difference!" I proclaimed as we did our about face and descended down our last hill for that day. "I agree," my dad nodded, "almost like we ran a completely different set of hills."

Anyone who has run with me long enough knows I get bored with running the same routes very quickly. I love adventure and running in new places. So it came as no surprise to my dad last summer when one morning I announced: "I just don't feel like running our short hill course today." We had been having a steady diet of this route for the last 2 months and I was growing weary of seeing the same hills, anticipating the same tough spots and land marks demarking how much further I had to go.

"We can certainly run a different course, but you will be sacrificing the progress these hills bring to your training," Dad commented. I knew he was right. He offered a suggestion: "How about we just run the course in reverse? Maybe a change of perspective will help."

After agreeing to this change in direction we were off to experience our short hills course again, as if for the first time. It was amazing the new life it breathed into our run. My old reference points were gone. My old anticipated struggle areas were removed. I noticed gradual inclines, up and down, in places I had never known before. Even subtle things like having the lake to our right side rather than our left, and the sun at our faces rather than our backs added a refreshing perspective to our every step as the hills ticked by. I found myself finding renewed energy as this new course rolled under my feet. I was enjoying the new perspective and having fun. Same course, different look, NEW FEEL!

During our cool down that day we discussed the cool change that had just taken place. We had run the exact same hills, distance and course as always. Our GPS position on the map had not changed. It was the simple change of running the course in reverse that brought a refreshing new experience to that morning's run. It was like looking at the course through a new lens, with no preconceived notions or expectations.

Like the old saying goes: "Variety is the spice of life!" After that run I came to understand the truth of that saying. Variety is a tonic for satisfying our inborn curiosity as human beings. We are geared for exploration, discovery and change. We are not creatures who find satisfaction in the "same old, same old." There is no joy in the rut!

That run opened my eyes to the importance of shaking things up every now and then. When I sense staleness creeping into my routine, I always flash back to the lesson of this run. I look for ways to alter my perspective by changing "what I am doing." Or sometimes it is simply changing "how I do" something--maybe even "how I think" about something that stimulates a sense of fresh excitement again.

AHAS:

> "Variety is the spice of life!"
>
> There is not much joy in a rut.
>
> We are geared for exploration, discovery and change.
>
> Same course, different look, NEW FEEL!

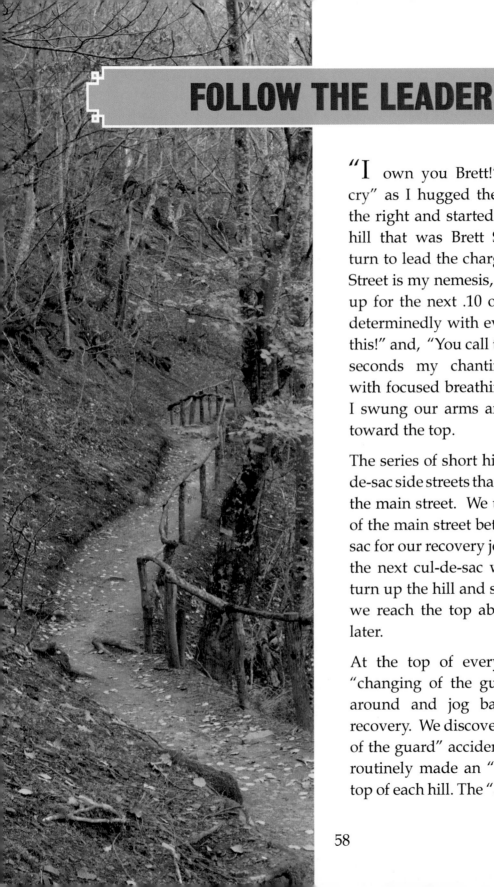

FOLLOW THE LEADER

"I own you Brett!" - was my "war cry" as I hugged the corner tightly to the right and started my ascent up the hill that was Brett Street. It was my turn to lead the charge, and since Brett Street is my nemesis, I was psyching us up for the next .10 of a mile, chanting determinedly with every step: "We got this!" and, "You call this a hill!" Within seconds my chanting was replaced with focused breathing as my dad and I swung our arms and drove our legs toward the top.

The series of short hills we run are cul-de-sac side streets that each connect with the main street. We use the flat section of the main street between each cul-de-sac for our recovery jog. Upon reaching the next cul-de-sac we make the right turn up the hill and start charging until we reach the top about 30-45 seconds later.

At the top of every hill we have a "changing of the guards" as we turn around and jog back down in our recovery. We discovered this "changing of the guard" accidently when we each routinely made an "about face" at the top of each hill. The "about face" caused

Leadership comes with the power to inspire. With the power to inspire comes the power to grow.

us to switch positions so that Dad, who was running on my right side going up the hill, was now on my left side when going back down. This shift of position is significant because it causes each one of us to run on the right side and assume the leadership position on every other hill. After discovering this switch we decided to turn it into a game of "Follow the Leader," and it has been one of my favorite parts of the workout ever since.

Here is how we play the game: the person running on the right side will be on the inside track as we round the corner to go up the hill. Running this "inside" position means that he/she will have the advantage of reaching the starting point of the uphill first and so assumes leadership on this hill. This runner sets the pace while the other runner on the outside has to work harder to match the pace and catch up. On occasion the lead runner's pace may start to falter and the follower will become the encourager

and push the pace from behind. This is called "leading from behind!" We play this game of tag throughout all 10 hill repeats. Exchanging leader and follower roles is like a social experiment we get to play out for a half hour every week.

Well, maybe "social experiment" is not the right term for the game....But here is what I mean: with the leadership role of the inside position the runner assumes increased responsibility and accountability for the quality of the workout during that brief period of time. This person has the obvious power of setting the pace but also must remain sensitive to the struggle of the follower trying to keep up. The first few seconds of the uphill are tough on the follower because the leader is charging and the follower feels like they are being dropped out the "back door of the bus." During these first few seconds the leader has the power to inspire or destroy. Pushing harder at this point may satisfy the ego of the leader but may destroy the will of the follower to carry on. To inspire, the leader must be sensitive to the struggle going on behind. Throttling the pace back accordingly and adding a few words of encouragement can help the follower dig deep to reestablish shoulder to shoulder position with the leader.

Playing this game has taught me that with the power of leadership comes the power to mislead. With the power to mislead comes the power to destroy. In those critical first few seconds of the hill the integrity of the workout hangs in the balance by two strands: accountability and motivation. The effective leader will remain accountable for maintaining a pace that corresponds with the goal of the workout and will also run with a spirit that motivates his/her teammate rather than conquers.

I have carried these insights from the hills into my life. I'm trying to be more aware of how I use the power I have with my children, friends and business relationships. I want to use my power in a way that inspires.

AHAS:

- Good leaders inspire people to achieve their potential:
  - By motivating them to achieve the goals they want.
  - By holding them accountable to do what they need to do.
- With the power of leadership comes the power to mislead. With the power to mislead comes the power to destroy.
- Leadership comes with the power to inspire. With the power to inspire comes the power to grow.

One more thing…

We are all leaders in the sense that we carry the responsibility to take care of and encourage one another through the hills of life. Joy in life is not about reaching the top at the exclusion of others, on the contrary, it is about reaching the top with others at our side. It is a lie to believe that the top of the hill is too crowded; there is plenty of room. So, when you are at the bottom of your hill and it is your turn to lead, extend both your hands and encourage someone to run up with you. The view at the top of the hill is always better when shared with others.

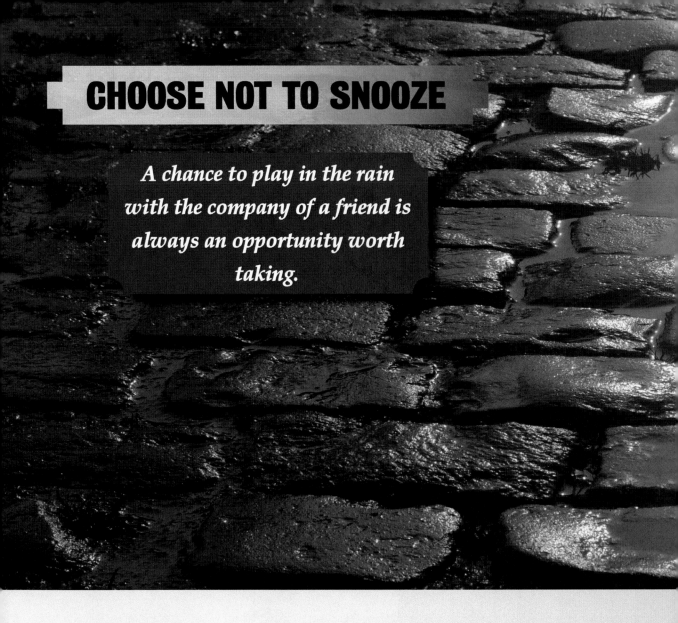

CHOOSE NOT TO SNOOZE

A chance to play in the rain with the company of a friend is always an opportunity worth taking.

I love waking up to the sound of rain lightly dancing across my rooftop, and the sound of the wind gently whipping its pellets into my windows. It is such a soothing sound that even on this "Daddy-Daughter Run" day I want to pull my covers back up over my ears and drift back to sleep. But who was I kidding; I knew my dad was lacing up his running shoes in eager anticipation of getting out and playing in the rain. As I turned over and wrapped the bed covers tighter, I began to recall fond memories of my teenage years in Oregon where my dad and I shared many rainy runs together. There is something about running through

the foggy dense mist which hovers over twisted fern lined trails that soothes my soul. It seems strangely primitive and haunting, and yet comforting all at the same time. Recounting those memories with covers wrapped tight, I began considering my options and realized that the quality of my life today would be determined by *what I appreciate and choose to experience*. On this rainy morning I could choose to have my day defined by hitting the snooze and skipping the run, or it could be defined by getting up and lacing my shoes for another "Daddy-Daughter Run" memory. I realized that making either choice would be okay. What mattered was

to make my decision according to what I appreciate most, sleeping or running, and how I want to define my life. In that moment I tossed back the covers and within minutes was out the door headed to meet my dad.

This morning's light drizzle was a welcome relief from the scorching heat of our typical Arkansas summer. Living plants of all varieties emerged from their wilting droop as they eagerly gulped the cooling moisture. We also found ourselves being refreshed by the drizzling shower soaking through our clothes and to our skin. We felt like we were "dancing in the rain" with Fred Astaire! Then everything changed when we came to our first hill. The oil slicked streets quickly turned our "dance" into a slippery "spin" and we were in for a challenge.

While the oil made it nearly impossible to gain traction, Mother Nature decided to turn the rain from drizzle into a downpour and we were not even half way yet! Spinning feet, heavy clothes, drowning downpour all combined to turn our play into work. This was tough!

One by one we dispatched each hill until finally we crested the top of our last one.

We did it! We slayed the "demons of quit" today! We fist bumped each other with a hearty sense of accomplishment.

Later that day I thought of the memory my dad and I built that morning. And I thought of how close I came to missing it if I would have chosen to stay under the covers. I am glad I made the choice I did. Was it challenging? Yes. Was it a little miserable? Yes. Was it worth it? Absolutely!

Looking back over the years I realize that some of my most memorable runs have been with friends in the rain, snow, mud, and other less than ideal situations. If I had chosen to hit the snooze button on those days I would have missed out on some of my most precious memories. In life, as in running, I am learning that difficulties and problems bring opportunities for me to learn and grow. Choosing to avoid challenges may be easier and more comfortable in the moment, but getting up and taking them on will produce the rich experiences that fill life with meaning.

AHAS

- ➤ Our quality of life is determined by what we *appreciate and choose* to experience.

- ➤ Opportunities to learn and grow come disguised as problems and difficulties.

- ➤ A chance to play in the rain with the company of a friend is always an opportunity worth taking.

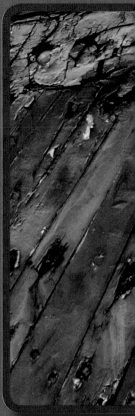

AUTO PILOT

Where your focus goes, your energy flows. - Where your energy flows determines your direction. Your direction determines your destination. Your destination determines your quality of life.

"Let's run them all!" I proclaimed as I walked in the back door of my dad's house. Maybe it was exposure to cold temperatures or the wind had blown something lose in my brain but I was proposing that we run all 18 hills on his side of the neighborhood. Our normal route only covers 10 of the hills with 1 hill on my side of the neighborhood for warm up. "I don't know" he responded hesitatingly..."but I guess we could give it a try." Who else's 60-year-old dad rallies to the challenge of 4 miles full of hill repeats? How cool is that?!

So, out the door we headed and proceeded to plan our strategy for this new workout. We decided that with the proposed change our usual warm up would not

be needed and we would just run the whole thing at our comfortable, controlled warm up pace. We would not be concerned with speed as we were not sure what kind of toll the added hills would take on us. This proved to be our "good call # 1" for the day (*This would be the first of 3 good calls we would make today.*)

Turning west, away from my dad's street, we started making our way towards the front entrance of the subdivision. As soon as we made the turn, we were instantly slapped in the face by a forceful gale of relentless wind--the kind you have to lean in to in order to maintain forward momentum. We felt like we had entered a wind tunnel and instantly took a sanity check: "are we up for this?" And then it dawned on us that we had unwittingly stumbled into our "good call #2." By heading west we only had to buck this wind for about 5 minutes until we reached the front entrance, where our first hill would begin. We would then turn around and head east; running all 18 hills to the back of the subdivision. "Heck yeah! With the wind at our back we can do this!"

What a relief it was to turn out of the wind and run up our first hill. I can't believe I am writing that I felt relieved running uphill! But it was a welcome change to get that biting wind out of our face. We exchanged the effort of leaning into the wind, to leaning into the hill. "There is #1 in the bag!," I proclaimed as we crested the top, and started our decent. "Yup, let's keep count," my dad chimed in as we settled into our downhill recovery stride.

#2, #3, #4, #5...we ticked 'em off one by one as we flew through the crisp morning air. The first 8 hills went by quickly with wind at our back and the occasional distraction of Christmas decorated houses along our route. As we approached hill #9 we both realized that half the workout was already behind us and we were cruising! And right there is where we made good call #3. Hill 9 marks the beginning of our usual workouts. It is where our legs are conditioned to start firing as we attack the hills, like race horses when starting gates are flung open. We both sensed our bodies shift into this attack mode as we rounded the corner and began our lean into the hill. Upon reaching the top we were stunned by our subconscious response as we counted "#9!" with a collective gasp. Realizing the shift that had just occurred, we deliberately refocused on our goal to run a comfortable controlled pace for this workout. We chuckled at how easy it is to lose focus and fall into old conditioned patterns.

#10, #11, #12, #13.....#18 ended with jelly legs and not an ounce of pep left in our step. If we had not caught ourselves on #9 and throttled back, I am not sure we could have finished all 18 hills without beating ourselves up. We definitely earned a well-deserved high-five for our "blue ribbon" focused effort.

During our cool down we discussed how critical it was that we made our adjustment, and how easy it is to get carried away and lose focus.

The same is true in life. Like a boat drifting with the current, it is easy to go through life on autopilot, reactively moving through our hills and valleys without realizing that we are drifting off course from our goals. We may find ourselves falling into old conditioned patterns because that is what feels comfortable. The problem is that if we always do what we have always done; we will always get what we have always gotten. It is like the definition of insanity: *"doing the same thing again and again, and expecting different results."* There are times when we need to refocus, grab the rudder and steer our boat away from currents that can harm us. Sometimes "going with the flow" can lead to destruction.

Today's 18 hills taught me the lesson of living with *purpose*. It is easy to drift; anybody can do that. And the thing about drifting is that it will usually take us where *someone else wants us to go*. Think about it. *If we do not keep focused on where we are going, we are liable to stray and follow where someone else is going.*

Success in life (as in running) comes with *focused* effort.

AHAS:

➤ Where your *focus goes*, your *energy flows*. - Where your *energy flows* determines your *direction*. Your *direction* determines your *destination*. Your *destination* determines your *quality of life*.

➤ If we always do what we have always done, we will always get what we have always gotten.

➤ If we do not keep focused on where we are going, we are liable to stray and follow where someone else is going.

*If
you do not
know where you
want
to go, any path will
take you there.*

WHAT DO I WANT

"If you do not have a specific goal then it does not matter what we run." My dad's words stopped me cold. I had called him to see if he had a workout in mind for tomorrow morning's run. He was right. Since returning from my Canadian running trip, I had not set any new running goals and had no direction for my training. I was going through my runs from day to day not knowing what I wanted to accomplish next. *"We will talk about setting some new goals in the morning,"* he said. *"Every competitive runner needs to have a purpose and an end in mind"*.

Come morning we chose to run the meandering wooded trails behind my parent's house. Meandering seemed to be the appropriate kind of run for a runner without a goal. Running through the wooded terrain, climbing over hills, descending into valleys, and skirting around beaver ponds proved to be the perfect setting for thinking about what I wanted to do next.

We talked about my current roles of being a mother, wife, and business owner. And we talked about my responsibilities and priorities associated with each role. We discussed my available time for training and realized that training for a marathon would be unrealistic. It would put my other higher priorities at risk and create added emotional tension. I knew I did not want that.

What made this run memorable has less to do with identifying a goal for myself and more to do with the process my dad guided me through to discover my goal. After helping me identify my top roles he used a farming metaphor that encouraged me to consider what kind of crop I wanted to harvest in each of my roles. He asked me to consider what kind of seeds I needed to be planting and the level of attention I needed to give each role so that I could enjoy the harvest I wanted. What fascinated me is how this process also helped me identify very clearly _what I did **not** want!_ I clearly did not want to jeopardize my relationships with my family, particularly my husband and children. And I clearly knew I did not want to put our business at risk because of my inattention to employee and

customer needs. These were not expendable roles! *Being clear on what I did not want led me through the back door to discover what I did want!*

Through this process I also came to understand the risk involved with drifting along without a goal over a prolonged period of time. I realized that without a goal of my own, I will be at risk of losing interest or assuming someone else's training program. I realized that I had already started doing this when I called my dad to see if he had a workout in mind. I came to understand a significant truth: *If I don't decide what I want, then someone else will decide for me!*

I will never forget the process of discovery I experienced on that meandering trail run. I eventually settled on a goal to run a half-marathon in the spring. It would require the blended training of speed and endurance that I like, and it would fit within my current life situation. Now I know what workout I am doing tomorrow!

AHAS:

- ➢ If you do not know where you want to go, any path will take you there.

- ➢ Decide what you want. If you do not know what you want, try thinking about what you do not want.

- ➢ If we do not decide what we want, someone else will decide for us.

ZINGS

My father is a man of many talents and a true inspiration to anyone he has ever worked with or coached. He is the kind of person that you just want to be around. I think it must be his blended experience as teacher, coach and chaplain that has a way of inspiring people to find meaning in their lives. Whenever I bump into a runner who has been coached by my dad, they frequently share memories of his positive influence in their lives.

I recall the time when my father had just recently conducted the funeral for the mother of one of our dear friends. The experience was obviously on his mind as we started our early morning warm-up. He shared how honored and privileged he felt to be trusted with conducting the ceremony. We continued exchanging rambling thoughts about life until the conclusion of our warm-up brought them to silence. As if on cue our back and forth banter gave way to the urgent call for focus.

It was a hot and humid morning, with a thick muggy haze that seemed to ooze from the pavement and create a steamy fog around our shins. It was the kind of oppressive humidity that feels heavy on your chest, creates a sweat slosh in your shoes, and turns clothing into wet washrags. This day would prove to mark a fine line between running and swimming, and I think we used the term "embrace the suck" at some point on every hill!

We were beasts on this day, creating fire from the heat as we blazed to a new PR (Personal Record). Our self-promised reward of plunging into the swimming pool

Let time teach you how very little of it we have here. Then treat every second of it as a treasure.

when finished kept us pushing to "get 'r done!" We were like two horses running for the barn with a bucket full of fresh crisp apples waiting for us.

Finally, we hit the pool and I swear I could hear the hiss of heat meeting cool at the water's surface. And this is where something magical happened. We soon found ourselves continuing our warm-up conversation about the funeral my father recently conducted. Only now he started to share his personal experience of precious memories about his father (my grandfather). He shared that since his father's passing, four years ago, he is occasionally moved by a scene, a song, a

scent, etc. that evokes a precious memory of his father. He said he calls these moments "ZINGS" because they come like a bolt of electricity into his heart, causing chill bumps and hair to rise. He shared how he never wants those moments to quit coming because when they come, it is almost as if his dad is right there with him in that moment. He said that he expects the ZINGS to keep coming without end because of the deep reservoir of relationship and experiences he shared with his dad. He went on to say that in the end it is not about bank accounts and houses and status; it is the shared experiences with loved ones that provide the resource material for the ZINGS. And as time passes it will be those occasional ZINGS that make life meaningful and rich.

At that moment I looked at my dad's face and noticed the small lines of age that had begun forming around his eyes, the wrinkling and slight loosening of skin on his neck and arms. I was overcome with sadness and gratitude all at once.

Sad with the realization that I too will one day only be able to experience the relationship with my father through a ZING, but also grateful that I have the opportunity every week to collect special moments for those ZINGS to come. I realized that at that very moment I was creating a ZING that will hit me some day after a long run when I jump in the pool to refresh. I will get a ZING, and then smile, remembering this day and knowing he is still there.

So with tears rolling down my face, as I type this, I beg you to go collect memories today, create some future ZINGS!!!

AHAS:

> Grab life with both hands, really experience it, live it and love it to its fullest.

> Let time teach you how very little of it we have here. Then treat every second of it as a treasure.

> Instead of collecting things, be a collector of *ZINGS!*

YOU ARE NOT YOUR RUN

"*Watch out! Be careful not to fall in that trap!*" These words of warning from my dad were spoken with such unusual intensity that I was immediately brought to attention and arrested from my funk.

My dad must have sensed my depressed mood as I shared my "woe is me" frustration with my recent discouraging race performance. I was disgusted that I had not achieved my goal after spending so much time and energy in training. As we continued running, I rambled on explaining my humiliation of posting such a poor time and losing to others whom I felt I shouldn't have. I was in the middle of a "pity party" and was inviting my dad to join. His words of warning were a flat out rejection of my invitation. For the next several minutes he alerted me to a potential blind spot and challenged my motivation for running.

"*Do not let what you do define who you are.*" He said. He continued with even more emphasis, "*You are not your run!*" He shared his experience of falling into this trap as a competitive runner and explained how destructive it is to get "*our doing mixed up with our being.*" I could tell that his passion was coming from a place of personal experience. He was sharing something very important, so I stopped my "pity party" and listened closely. By the end of the run I had experienced a paradigm shift, which has totally liberated newfound joy in my running life. Here is a summary of what I heard:

- If our value is based.upon what we do, then we are setting ourselves up to be miserable when we do not perform according to our expectation.

- If running becomes a means to validate our worth, it will eventually betray us because there will always be someone who can run faster.

- If our running performance is the measure of our self-respect then as each year goes by, our self-respect will fade along with our aging body.

- Because we are human and prone to making mistakes, our dignity should never be dependent on what we do or based on other's judgment. Dignity is to the soul as air and food are to the body. Leaving our dignity vulnerable to

our human frailty and others' judgments exposes us to possible emotional starvation and suffocation. If we sense that we are losing our dignity, (self-respect, value, and worth) we will become consumed with reclaiming it; even at the expense of our health and possible exclusion of others.

I finished that "*Daddy-Daughter Run*" with a completely different perspective of where running fits in my life. I realized that my running was becoming alarmingly close to defining my identity. I was treating it as something bigger than it is and it had started consuming me. I am glad my dad recognized it and called it out for me. Since then I have put my passion for running into its rightful place: It is recreation. It is a game. **It is fun. It is something I do, not who I am!**

AHAS:

> Running is something I do, NOT WHO I AM!

THE GREATEST ADVENTURE EVER

*Do not let the regrets of the
past or the worries of the future
betray the gift of the present!*

Putting on my running shoes one particular Thursday morning I noticed this amazing glow coming through my bathroom window. As I pulled back the curtains, I was greeted with the piercing beauty of the sun cresting up over the lake. The pink cotton-candy-like hues seemed to engulf everything as the sun stretched out its rays to take its perch in the sky. Watching dawn break always excites me as it unfolds its promise of a new day and new opportunities to embrace and experiences to cherish as they become part of my life's adventure. On this morning I was in particular awe of its beauty and was instantly filled with a sense of gratitude that I was given the gift of running; that I have this time to lace up my running shoes, head out my door and experience such a beautiful sunrise with my father by my side. Walking across the bridge to the other side of the lake toward my parent's house, I stared out over the lake and watched the geese slowly glide into the glass-still water, highlighted with pink feathers from the sun's glow. I reflected back upon my years of running with my father and the many special moments we have shared along the way. As I paused on the bridge to take in the warmth of the morning, I was struck by the gift of the present moment as a new day unfolded before me with its endless possibilities.

As I continued standing there, I began to replay a recent conversation with a very dear friend that changed my life forever, and helped me to see the beauty in moments like these. It was after a long trail run and I was sharing with him what my husband's and my life would be like once our kids had grown up and he could retire. How we would travel and experience the world. What my friend said in response was a game changer for me. He simply asked, "Why are you wishing your lives away, waiting to live in some other time period that you are not even promised?" He was so right! Life is happening now. Happiness is not some future endeavor, but a present reality. We have to be ever mindful to cultivate happiness in our life and the lives of the people we know and love right now. This present moment is what we are given, and the collection of these

moments is ultimately what writes the chapters in the book of our lives. I don't know about you but at the end of my days I want to look back on my book and read the story of a great adventure, a life lived and loved fully. A story that was not afraid to go through plot twists when necessary, full of risks taken, people loved and countless memories collected. I want there to be chapters with some heartache, bumps and bruises and even some regrets proving that I was moving forward and strengthening my character. It may not be a New York Times best-seller or gain any flashy awards, but it will be a manuscript that I will be proud of, lived with integrity to my values and the rich fullness of a great adventure.

Leaving the bridge and this incredible scene behind, I thought how refreshing it is to be fully engaged in the present, like taking a deep breath of fresh air. In the distance, at the base of the hill, I noticed my dad gazing out over the lake taking in the glorious scene as well. I realized it was time to step into the next moment and go write another Daddy-Daughter Run chapter! I want to live life in a way that when it is over, it will be "fist bump" worthy. I want to live it so that I will be able to high five my partners, slap them on the butt and say: **"That was The Greatest Adventure Ever!"**

Ahas:

➤ Do not let the regrets of the past or the worries of the future betray the gift of the present!

➤ Live life in a way that when it is over, it will be "fist bump" worthy. Live it so that you will be able to high five your partners, slap them on the butt and say:

"That was THE GREATEST ADVENTURE EVER!"

AFTERWORD

Thank you for buying and reading our book. We hope you found it worth your time and money. We would like to hear your thoughts about it. Please take a moment and log into the online retailer you purchased our book from. We would appreciate your honest review of our book, as this will help us in future endeavors.

Our desire is to inspire and encourage others to live their lives powerfully. Inevitably, we all encounter challenges that test our ability to persevere and sometimes we are blindsided by "hills" that rock our world and cause our knees to buckle. No matter what hill we find ourselves climbing (be it a financial problem, loss of a job, struggling marriage, or loss of health, etc.) each one can cause us to feel insufficient and weak. They can overwhelm us to the point of giving up.

Our experience has shown us that it is in the company of others that we become energized to live powerfully. We believe our success has been directly related to our willingness to ask for help and engage with others. That is why choosing "**We Run Up!**" as the title of our book seemed so appropriate.

We hope this book will inspire you to live your life powerfully in the face of adversity. No matter what kind of hill you encounter we hope these pages will encourage you to find the resiliency and strength you need by asking others to "RUN UP" with you.

THE WORKOUT THAT INSPIRED THE BOOK SHORT HILLS

This is the workout we used to start our "Daddy-Daughter Day" runs. And ultimately it is where we became inspired to write the "We Run Up!" book.

BENEFITS:

> Strengthen lower leg (calf muscles) which will in turn improve stride length. Improved stride length will promote faster running.

> Helps the runner focus on maintaining efficient running form.

(Note: This is great training to do in the winter and will promote faster running in the spring.)

HOW TO PLAY WITH SHORT HILLS:

Find a hill that is more steeply graded than gentle. Be careful though; you want a challenging hill, but not too steep. Running to the top of this hill should take you about 30-45 seconds.

> Warm up with 1-2 miles easy jog on the flat (no hills) followed by light stretching.

➤ Run 10 TIMES uphill at 85% effort. This should feel explosive with arms swinging, toes pushing off, and knees lifting. Be careful not to lose your form. The temptation will be to cast your eyes downward so that you are looking at your feet. This will cause you to hunch your back and will restrict your breathing. Keeping your eyes focused on the top of the hill will lift your head and enable your chest to thrust forward *(Imagine a rope attached to your chest and you are being pulled up the hill)*. Upon reaching the top, cut your effort to easy recovery pace and jog easily back down the hill. Continue jogging when reaching the bottom until you are recovered a total of 60-90 seconds. After the recovery phase is complete, run back up the hill again.

➤ Cool down with 1-2 miles easy jog / walk.

Beginner: 3-4 TIMES uphill every other week.

Intermediate: 5-7 TIMES uphill every other week

Advanced: 10-12 TIMES uphill every other week (or once every 10 days)

"AHAS" QUICK REFERENCE

WE STRIVE TOGETHER

- ➤ Do not let the start stop you!

- ➤ Life is not an individual sport; it is a team adventure!

- ➤ The degree to which we experience success in life is the degree to which we are willing to ask for help!

- ➤ The Latin root of the word "compete" is com petere, meaning "to strive together."

KEEP IT FUN

- ➤ We play harder than we work.

- ➤ Our thinking and speaking directly affect our level of energy and enthusiasm.

WHERE THE GRASS IS GREENER

- ➤ We betray the authenticity of our experience and potential when we compare ourselves to others and try to live according to their style.

- ➤ The grass is not always greener on the other side, it is greener where we water it!

WHAT WAS I THINKING

- ➤ Failing to prepare is preparing to fail.

- ➤ Passionate desire is the spark that ignites the fire to persevere and do the disciplined work of preparation.

- ➤ The willingness to prepare is more important than the desire to succeed.

We Run Up!

BELIEVE IT TO SEE IT

- Belief is the glue makes commitment to stick.
- My believing precedes my achieving.
- Belief is the catalyst that gets us started and the motor that keeps us moving.

ONE MORE AND THEN ONE MORE

- Mile by mile can feel like a trial, but inch by inch will make it a cinch.
- Problems filled our plate one at a time and can be most effectively removed in the same manner.
- Remember the concept of how to eat an elephant; one bite at a time!

SUCCESS COMES IN A CAN

- Success comes in a can, not in a "can't!"
- More important than what you have or do not have, is what you do with what you have!

98

LESSONS OF THE FARM

- ➤ Our joy is found not so much in the destination as it is in the process of getting there.

- ➤ What we overcome is often more important than what we accomplish.

- ➤ It is in the patient struggle of the seed pushing through the soil that makes breaking through such a triumph!

BAGGAGE

- ➤ Just because someone says something about me, does not mean it is true.

- ➤ Saying, "No" is easy when I have a bigger "Yes" in mind.

- ➤ I will not allow my dreams to be held hostage to someone else's expectation of me.

- ➤ My value as a person is not symbolized by "stuff."

PERSPECTIVE

- Variety is the spice of life!

- There is not much joy in a rut.

- We are geared for exploration, discovery and change.

- Same course, different look, new feel!

FOLLOW THE LEADER

- Good leaders inspire people to achieve their potential;

  - By motivating them to achieve the goals they want.

  - By holding them accountable to do what they need to do.

- With the power of leadership comes the power to mislead. With the power to mislead comes the power to destroy.

- Leadership comes with the power to inspire. With the power to inspire comes the power to grow.

CHOOSE NOT TO SNOOZE

- Our quality of life is determined by what we appreciate and choose to experience.

- Opportunities to learn and grow come disguised as problems and difficulties.

- A chance to play in the rain with the company of a friend is always an opportunity worth taking.

AUTO PILOT

- Where your focus goes, your energy flows.

- Where your energy flows determines your direction.

- Your direction determines your destination.

- Your destination determines your quality of life.

- ➤ If we always do what we have always done; we will always get what we have always gotten.

- ➤ If we do not keep focused on where we are going, we are liable to stray and follow where someone else is going.

WHAT DO I WANT

- ➤ If you don't know where you want to go, any path will take you there.

- ➤ Decide what you want. If you do not know what you want, try thinking about what you do not want.

- ➤ If we do not decide what we want, someone else will decide for us.

ZINGS

- ➤ Grab life with both hands, really experience it, live it and love it to the fullest.

- ➤ Let time teach you how very little of it we have here. Then treat every second of it as a treasure.

- ➤ Instead of collecting things, be a collector of Zings!

YOU ARE NOT YOUR RUN

- ➤ Running is something I do, not who I am!

THE GREATEST ADVENTURE EVER

- ➤ Do not let the regrets of the past or the worries of the future betray the gift of the present.

- ➤ Live life in a way that when it is over, it will be "fist bump" worthy. Live it so that you will be able to high five your partners, slap them on the butt and say, " That was the greatest adventure ever!"

ANDREA
SAYERS

ABOUT THE AUTHORS

Andrea Sayers has been involved with running and fitness ever since she was a little child. Some of her earliest memories include watching her father running on the track. She would play in the infield sand or tag along either on foot or bike as her dad logged numerous training miles. Because of that, her passion for fitness is ingrained in her and her goal is always to spread that passion and commitment for a healthy lifestyle to as many people as possible. Her background includes personal training individuals and groups, helping with nutrition needs and, in general, impacting lives in a positive, meaningful way. Andrea started personal training about 13 years ago, running a small personal training studio out of her house and, ultimately, owning a fitness facility in Cabot, Arkansas. Prevail Fitness, the gym she owns, has opened many doors, including; working with local celebrities, making weekly appearances on a local radio station to share fitness tips, hosting multiple 5K races, doing public speaking engagements and fundraisers and, most importantly, allowing her to advocate the need to lead a healthy lifestyle on a much larger scale. She now shares her passion through blogs ranging from running, to plant-based athletes, health and fitness, to natural beauty and vegan cooking. You can access those blogs and keep up with the latest books she is writing at **andreasayers.com** and **werunup.com**. Also, follow her on Facebook at **https://www.facebook.com/AndreaSayersPrevailFitness** and **https://www.facebook.com/weruncommunity**.

DENNIS REEDER

DENNIS REEDER

Dennis Reeder lives in Cabot, Arkansas where he and his wife Jan are enjoying active retirement. They are the parents of two children, and proud grandparents of seven. Aside from his varied hobbies of running, golfing, fishing, cycling, and hiking, Dennis works part time as an Independent Contractor teaching positive youth development in the local public schools. His teaching draws life from his diverse career experience as a small business owner, corporate trainer for Nike, Inc., and most recent Certification as Clinical Chaplain. Dennis is a teacher at heart. When he's out of the class room you will often find him using his teaching skills as a golf instructor or long distance running coach.

We Run Up!